# My Dog's Life
## Scrapbook and Journal

## Yorkshire Terrier

Capture the special moments!

*Until one has loved a dog a part*
*of one's heart remains unawakened*

A dog journal scrapbook to
document your dog's life as it happens!

*Puppies and dogs are earthly miracles with wagging tails,
little hearts full of love and the pitter-patter of paws.*

# A Dog Journal and Scrapbook

A journal and scrapbook for your dog to keep heart filled memories and photos of special moments with your dog. There is space for lots of snapshots of your dog! This blank memory book gives dog lovers a place to chart their dog's growth.

As your dog grows into an adult you can create a book full of memories and capture the special moments.

There is a page for your dog's first birthday, first Christmas, first bath plus birth information. Keep track of your dog's vaccine records and health.

There is even a page to place your dog's paw prints!

You can take photos of your dog discovering his world as he grows into an adult.

Pictures are worth a thousand words, it helps us remember the little moments that bring us such joy in an instant.

Don't miss the special times when your dog is sleeping, bounding across the yard, their first birthday or favorite things to do! With this dog memory book you will be able to keep your favorite memories to enjoy the happy moments for years!

Start creating lasting memories today of your puppy or dog!

*Yesterday I was a dog. Today I'm a dog.*
*Tomorrow I'll probably still be a dog.*
*Sigh! There's so little hope for advancement.*

*~Charles M. Schulz*

# My First Day Home

Date I joined my new family: ______________________

*My First Selfie*

| |
|---|
| Photo Here |

# My First Week Home

My Birthday: ______________________________

Place of Birth: ______________________________

Fur and Markings: ___________________________

My Name: ________________________________

**I'm growing. How much did I grow!**

| Age | Lbs | Oz |
|---|---|---|
| 6 Weeks | | |
| 8 Weeks | | |
| 10 Weeks | | |
| 3 Months | | |
| 4 Months | | |
| 6 Months | | |
| 8 Months | | |
| 10 Months | | |
| 1 Year | | |
| 2 Years | | |

## Puppy Paw Print

## Adult Paw Print

# My Favorite Person

Photo Here

## My First Bath

Photo Here

# My Favorite Food

Photo Here

# My Favorite Toy

Photo Here

# My First Birthday

Photo Here

# My First Christmas

Photo Here

# Vaccination Records

| Age | Date | Distemper | Parvo | Rabies | Deworm |
|---|---|---|---|---|---|
| 6 weeks | | | | | |
| 10 weeks | | | | | |
| 14 weeks | | | | | |
| 1 Year | | | | | |
| 2 Years | | | | | |
| 3 Years | | | | | |
| 4 Years | | | | | |
| 5 Years | | | | | |
| 6 Years | | | | | |
| 7 Years | | | | | |
| 8 Years | | | | | |
| 9 Years | | | | | |
| 10 Years | | | | | |
| 11 Years | | | | | |
| 12 Years | | | | | |

## Heartworm Testing:

1 Year___ 2 Year___ 3 Year ___ 4 Year___ 5 Year___

6 Year___ 7 Year___ 8 Year ___ 9 Year___ 10 Year___

# Medical Record Notes:

# Medical Record Notes:

## Medical Record Notes:

# Medical Record Notes:

# Medical Treatments:

| Neutered | Spayed | Other |
| --- | --- | --- |
| | | |

# Medical Conditions:

| Date | Accidents or Injuries |
| --- | --- |
| | |
| | |
| | |
| | |
| | |
| | |
| | |
| | |
| | |
| | |
| | |
| | |
| | |
| | |
| | |
| | |

# Medical Emergencies:

## Medical Emergencies:

## The Puppy Days

The journey of a single memory starts with a photo!
Create lasting memories today!

# Our Adorable Puppy

Photo Here

# Our Adorable Puppy

Photo Here

# Our Adorable Puppy

Photo Here

# Our Adorable Puppy

Photo Here

# Our Adorable Puppy

Photo Here

# Our Adorable Puppy

Photo Here

# Our Adorable Puppy

Photo Here

# Our Adorable Puppy

Photo Here

# Our Adorable Puppy

Photo Here

# Our Adorable Puppy

Photo Here

# Our Adorable Puppy

Photo Here

# Our Adorable Puppy

Photo Here

# Our Adorable Puppy

Photo Here

# Our Adorable Puppy

Photo Here

# Our Adorable Puppy

Photo Here

# Our Adorable Puppy

Photo Here

# Our Adorable Puppy

Photo Here

# Our Adorable Puppy

Photo Here

# Our Adorable Puppy

Photo Here

# Our Adorable Puppy

Photo Here

# Our Adorable Puppy

Photo Here

# Our Adorable Puppy

Photo Here

# Our Adorable Puppy

Photo Here

# Our Adorable Puppy

Photo Here

# Our Adorable Puppy

Photo Here

# Our Adorable Puppy

Photo Here

# Our Adorable Puppy

Photo Here

# Our Adorable Puppy

Photo Here

# Our Adorable Puppy

Photo Here

# Our Adorable Puppy

Photo Here

# Our Adorable Puppy

Photo Here

# Our Adorable Puppy

Photo Here

# Our Adorable Puppy

Photo Here

# Our Adorable Puppy

Photo Here

# Our Adorable Puppy

Photo Here

# Our Adorable Puppy

Photo Here

## All Grown Up

Don't miss the special moments!
The journey of a single memory starts with a photo!

# All Grown Up

Photo Here

# All Grown Up

Photo Here

# All Grown Up

Photo Here

# All Grown Up

Photo Here

# All Grown Up

Photo Here

# All Grown Up

Photo Here

# All Grown Up

Photo Here

# All Grown Up

Photo Here

# All Grown Up

Photo Here

# All Grown Up

Photo Here

# All Grown Up

Photo Here

# All Grown Up

Photo Here

# All Grown Up

Photo Here

# All Grown Up

Photo Here

# All Grown Up

Photo Here

# All Grown Up

Photo Here

# All Grown Up

Photo Here

# All Grown Up

Photo Here

# All Grown Up

Photo Here

# All Grown Up

Photo Here

# All Grown Up

Photo Here

# All Grown Up

Photo Here

# All Grown Up

Photo Here

# All Grown Up

Photo Here

# All Grown Up

Photo Here

# All Grown Up

Photo Here

# All Grown Up

Photo Here

# All Grown Up

Photo Here

# All Grown Up

Photo Here

# All Grown Up

Photo Here

# All Grown Up

Photo Here

# All Grown Up

Photo Here

# All Grown Up

Photo Here

# All Grown Up

Photo Here

# All Grown Up

Photo Here

# All Grown Up

Photo Here

# All Grown Up

Photo Here

# All Grown Up

Photo Here

Made in the USA
Las Vegas, NV
10 May 2021

22788523R00059